ART FROM ALASKA

ANCHORAGE MUSEUM AT RASMUSON CENTER

Pomegranate

SAN FRANCISCO

Pomegranate Communications, Inc.
Box 808022, Petaluma CA 94975
800 227 1428; www.pomegranate.com

Pomegranate Europe Ltd.
Unit 1, Heathcote Business Centre, Hurlbutt Road
Warwick, Warwickshire CV34 6TD, UK
[+44] 0 1926 430111; sales@pomeurope.co.uk

ISBN 978-0-7649-4203-7
Pomegranate Catalog No. AA415

Pomegranate publishes books of postcards on a wide range of subjects.
Please contact the publisher for more information.

Cover designed by Lora Santiago
Printed in Korea

16 15 14 13 12 11 10 09 08 07   10 9 8 7 6 5 4 3 2 1

To facilitate detachment of the postcards from this book, fold each card along its perforation line before tearing.

The Anchorage Museum opened in 1968, and since then its permanent collection has gone from a mere five paintings to over 22,000 objects. It serves the local community and visitors alike by showcasing the rich cultural history and art of Alaska.

Compiled from the collections of the Anchorage Museum, *Art from Alaska* surveys the wide range of art that has been created to celebrate and document the land, the wildlife, and the people who have lived in this rugged and beautiful place. You will find an Eskimo portrait by Native artist James Kivetoruk Moses, a sweeping vista of Mount McKinley by beloved Alaskan painter Sydney Mortimer Laurence, and a sleeping polar bear by Fred Machetanz. Glaciers, walruses, village scenes, and the northern lights are represented, from artists such as Jules Dahlager, Florence Nupok Malewotkuk, David Mollett, Eliot O'Hara, George Aden Ahgupuk, Carl Saxild, Wuanita Smith, and Prescott M. M. Jones.

These works together capture the essence of Alaska, a vast, dynamic land where mountains meet the sea and old cultures meet new—and where artists will always find inspiration.

ART FROM ALASKA

George Aden Ahgupuk (1911–2001)
Radio Babies, n.d.

Ink and watercolor on skin, 25 x 38 cm (9¹³⁄₁₆ x 14¹⁵⁄₁₆ in.)
Gift of National Bank of Alaska, 70.169.1

BOX 808022 PETALUMA CA 94975

Pomegranate

ART FROM ALASKA

Edwin Boyd Johnson (1904–1968)
Mount Kimball, Alaska, 1938

Oil on canvas, 76.7 x 102 cm (30³⁄₁₆ x 40³⁄₁₆ in.)
Joint purchase, Anchorage Museum Association and
Municipal Acquisition Fund, 92.78.1

BOX 808022   PETALUMA   CA 94975

Pomegranate

ART FROM ALASKA

Bernard Tuglamena Katexac (1922–1997)
Walruses, 1969

Woodblock print, 29 x 45.7 cm (11⁷⁄₁₆ x 18 in.)
Municipal Acquisition Fund purchase, 70.152.6

BOX 808022 PETALUMA CA 94975

Pomegranate

ART FROM ALASKA

James Kivetoruk Moses (1900–1982)
Untitled (Eskimo Men and Woman), c. 1950

Watercolor, pen, and ink on poster board,
30.7 x 45.6 cm (12¹⁄₁₆ x 17¹⁵⁄₁₆ in.)
Gift of Anchorage Museum Association, 87.29.2

BOX 808022   PETALUMA   CA 94975

Pomegranate

ART FROM ALASKA

Sydney Mortimer Laurence (1865–1940)
Aurora Borealis, n.d.

Oil on canvas, 41 x 51 cm (16⅛ x 20⅛ in.)
Gift of Freda M. Huncke of Leawood, Kansas, in memory of her early
life in Alaska, 95.75.06

CA 94975

PETALUMA

BOX 808022

Pomegranate

ART FROM ALASKA

Henry Wood Elliott (1846–1930)
The Fur Seal Millions, 1872

Watercolor on paper, 31.8 x 57.2 cm (12½ x 22½ in.)
Gift of Anchorage Museum Association, 87.48.1

BOX 808022   PETALUMA   CA 94975

Pomegranate

ART FROM ALASKA

Sydney Mortimer Laurence (1865–1940)
Silent Pool, n.d.

Oil on canvas, 52 x 41 cm (20½ x 16⅛ in.)
Gift of Anchorage Museum Association, 78.2

BOX 808022 PETALUMA CA 94975

Pomegranate

ART FROM ALASKA

Florence Nupok Malewotkuk (1906–1971)
Walrus on Ice Floe, c. 1965

Ink on sealskin, 104.1 x 134.5 cm (41 x 52¹⁵⁄₁₆ in.)
Gift of Anchorage Museum Association, 75.56.1

BOX 808022   PETALUMA   CA 94975

Pomegranate

ART FROM ALASKA

Prescott M. M. Jones (1904–1981)
Street in Ketchikan, 1937

Watercolor on paper, 57 x 78.7 cm (22⁷⁄₁₆ x 31 in.)
Municipal Acquisition Fund purchase, 79.80.2

BOX 808022   PETALUMA   CA 94975

Pomegranate

ART FROM ALASKA

Sydney Mortimer Laurence (1865–1940)
Mount McKinley, 1913

Oil on canvas, 50 x 76.5 cm (19¹¹⁄₁₆ x 30⅛ in.)
Gift of Anchorage Museum Association and Friends of
Anchorage Museum, 88.39.1

BOX 808022 PETALUMA CA 94975

Pomegranate

ART FROM ALASKA

Wuanita Smith (1866–1959)
The Chase, c. 1925

Color woodblock print, 30.5 x 24 cm (12 x 9⁷⁄₁₆ in.)
Gift of Anchorage Museum Association, 88.3.1

BOX 808022   PETALUMA   CA 94975

Pomegranate

ART FROM ALASKA

Eliot O'Hara (1890–1969)
Cape Saint Elias, Alaska, 1940–1941

Watercolor on paper, 40 x 53.4 cm (15¾ x 21 in.)
Gift of Anchorage Museum Association, 74.62.2

BOX 808022 PETALUMA CA 94975

Pomegranate

ART FROM ALASKA

Louise Lewis Gilbert (1900–1987)
Alaska Fisher Women, 1935

Oil on canvas, 87.3 x 102 cm (34⅜ x 40³⁄₁₆ in.)
Gift of Anchorage Museum Association, 87.54.1

BOX 808022   PETALUMA   CA 94975

Pomegranate

ART FROM ALASKA

Merlin F. Pollock (1905–1995)
Untitled (Fishing Docks), c. 1930

Watercolor on paper, 56 x 72 cm (22 1/16 x 28 3/8 in.)
Gift of Anchorage Museum Foundation, 2003.17.25

BOX 808022   PETALUMA   CA 94975

Pomegranate

Sell your books at
sellbackyourBook.com!
Go to sellbackyourBook.com
and get an instant price
quote. We even pay the
shipping - see what your old
books are worth today!

Inspected By: maura_sierra

00065866648

6648

c-2
S-2

0006586

ART FROM ALASKA

Frederick S. Dellenbaugh (1853–1935)
Log Houses, Kodiak Village, 1899

Oil on board, 13.5 x 22.2 cm (5⁵⁄₁₆ x 8¾ in.)
Gift of Mr. and Mrs. Elmer E. Rasmuson, 77.62.9

BOX 808022   PETALUMA   CA 94975

Pomegranate

ART FROM ALASKA

Fred Machetanz (1908–2002)
Mighty Hunter, 1967

Oil on board, 80.9 x 121.9 cm (31⅞ x 48 in.)
Gift of Moe Kadish, Atwood Foundation, Rasmuson Foundation,
Paul Boriak, Duty Free Shops of North America,
Norman E. Sommers, and Anchorage Municipal Acquisition Fund,
1982.108.001

BOX 808022   PETALUMA   CA 94975

Pomegranate

ART FROM ALASKA

David Mollett (b. 1950)
Carnivore Creek, 1988

Alkyd on canvas, 121.3 x 153.5 cm (47¾ x 60⁷⁄₁₆ in.)
Gift of Anchorage Museum Association, 1989.6.1

BOX 808022   PETALUMA   CA 94975

Pomegranate

ART FROM ALASKA

Fred Machetanz (1908–2002)
Quest for Avuk, 1973

Oil on board, 81.3 x 130.8 cm (32 x 51½ in.)
Gift of Mr. and Mrs. Elmer E. Rasmuson, 74.47.1

BOX 808022   PETALUMA   CA 94975

Pomegranate

ART FROM ALASKA

James Everett Stuart (1852–1941)
Extreme End of Indian Town, Sitka, Alaska, 1891

Oil on canvas, 61 x 106.4 cm (24 x 41⅞ in.)
Joint purchase, Anchorage Museum Association and Municipal
Acquisition Fund, 74.7.1

BOX 808022   PETALUMA   CA 94975

Pomegranate

ART FROM ALASKA

Thomas Hill (1829–1908)
Muir Glacier, 1889

Oil on canvas, 154.9 x 241.2 cm (61 x 94 15/16 in.)
Joint purchase, Anchorage Museum Association and
Municipal Acquisition Fund, 76.50.1

BOX 808022   PETALUMA   CA 94975

Pomegranate

ART FROM ALASKA

Magnus Colcord (Rusty) Heurlin (1895–1986)
After Fishing, c. 1960

Oil on board, 65.5 x 105.7 cm (25¹³⁄₁₆ x 41⅝ in.)
Gift of Rasmuson Foundation, 85.27.1

BOX 808022   PETALUMA   CA 94975

Pomegranate

ART FROM ALASKA

Jules Dahlager (1884–1952)
Deer Mountain, Cordova, n.d.

Oil on board, 20.3 x 15.2 cm (8 x 6 in.)
Gift of Mike and Becky Dahlager, 91.51.8

BOX 808022   PETALUMA   CA 94975

Pomegranate

ART FROM ALASKA

Cleveland S. Rockwell (1837–1907)
Untitled (View of Sitka), c. 1884

Watercolor on paper, 34.9 x 49.8 cm (13¾ x 19⅝ in.)
Gift of Anchorage Museum Association, 86.24.1

BOX 808022   PETALUMA   CA 94975

Pomegranate

ART FROM ALASKA

Jules Dahlager (1884–1952)
Power Creek, Cordova, Alaska, 1928

Oil on board, 17.8 x 12.7 cm (7 x 5 in.)
Gift of Rasmuson Foundation, 71.171.4

BOX 808022   PETALUMA   CA 94975

Pomegranate

ART FROM ALASKA

Carl Saxild (1893–1971)
Untitled (Northern Lights), c. 1925

Oil on canvas, 147.5 x 274 cm (58⅟₁₆ x 107⅞ in.)
Gift of Alaska Railroad Corporation, 1986.077.007

BOX 808022 PETALUMA CA 94975

Pomegranate

ART FROM ALASKA

Theodore J. Richardson (1855–1914)
Untitled (Wrangell Indian Village), c. 1900

Watercolor on board, 25 x 35 cm (9¹³⁄₁₆ x 13¾ in.)
Gift of Rasmuson Foundation, 74.52.1

BOX 808022   PETALUMA   CA 94975

Pomegranate

ART FROM ALASKA

William Seltzer Rice (1873–1963)
Indian Village, Alaska, c. 1930

Color woodblock print on Japanese paper,
24 x 19.2 cm (9⁷⁄₁₆ x 7⁹⁄₁₆ in.)
Joint purchase, Anchorage Museum Association and Municipal
Acquisition Fund, 91.22.1

BOX 808022   PETALUMA   CA 94975

Pomegranate

ART FROM ALASKA

Carl Saxild (1893–1971)
Untitled (Southeast Alaska Landscape), c. 1937

Oil on canvas, 102 x 132 cm (40³⁄₁₆ x 51¹⁵⁄₁₆ in.)
Gift of Alaska Railroad Corporation, 86.77.3

BOX 808022 PETALUMA CA 94975

Pomegranate

ART FROM ALASKA

Richard Peter Smith (c. 1855–?)
Untitled (USS Jamestown *at Sitka),* 1880

Oil on canvas, 40.7 x 71.5 cm (16 x 28⅛ in.)
Joint purchase, Anchorage Museum Association and
Municipal Acquisition Fund, 90.32.1

BOX 808022 PETALUMA CA 94975

Pomegranate

ART FROM ALASKA

Fred Machetanz (1908–2002)
Where Men and Dogs Seem Small, 1981

Oil on board, 79.8 x 64.7 cm (31⅞₆ x 25½ in.)
Gift of Jack and Gertrude Conway, 97.3.1

BOX 808022   PETALUMA   CA 94975

Pomegranate